Makin

Contents

written by Rachel Walker

author

The person who writes the story is called the author.

The author has to have
a good idea for a story.

3

The person who gets the story ready is called the publisher.

publisher

The publisher reads the story to see if it will make a good book.

designer

The person who plans the book is the designer. She has a good idea for how it will look.

editor

The person who checks the story is the editor. She reads the story to see if it is just right.

7

artist

The person who draws the pictures is the artist.

8

computer

Some artists make pictures on a computer.

The designer puts the story
and the pictures together.

checking

The editor and the publisher
check that it is ready.

printer

The person who makes the book is called the printer.

The printer makes a copy
for the publisher to check.

printing

Then the printer makes lots of copies of the book on big machines.

The publisher sells the books to stores and schools and libraries.

Children can read about how books are made. Happy reading!